IMAGES OF ENGLAND

ACOCKS GREEN

IMAGES OF ENGLAND

ACOCKS GREEN

MICHAEL BYRNE

First published 1997 by Tempus Publishing Ltd
Reprinted 1999, 2004, 2006, 2019

Reprinted in 2008 by
The History Press Ltd
97 St George's Place, Cheltenham,
Gloucestershire, GL50 3QB
www.thehistorypress.co.uk

British Library Cataloguing in Publication Data.
A catalogue record for this book is available from the British Library.

ISBN 978 0 7524 1039 5

Typesetting and origination by Tempus Publishing Limited.
Printed in Great Britain. by TJ International Ltd, Padstow, Cornwall.

Contents

Acknowledgements

In this book, thirty percent of the photographs come from either the Central Library, Acocks Green Library, or my own collection. The rest come from many sources. I would like to mention Frank Wells, Dianne Kenny, Karl Thomas, Peter White, John Bick and Mike Wood. The writings of C.J.G. Hudson, Victor Skipp, Vivian Bird, Joe McKenna and Frances Wilmot have been useful, as has the extensive collection of photocopies and books at Acocks Green Library: thanks to my colleague Brenda Clarke for her assistance with this material. Other printed sources are too numerous to mention. I would also like to thank Toni Demidowicz and Kevan Harrison from the Conservation Group of the city's Department of Planning and Architecture, Joan Holtham from the City Terrier, Diana Lay from Bass, Annette Albutt of the Diocesan Schools Commission, Revd Richard Postill from St Mary's church, Gareth Hickey from Birmingham Colour Lab, and Klick Photopoint for their help. My most heartfelt thanks must go to Les and Mary Smith of Acocks Green History Society, however. This book would be much the poorer without the kindness and generosity they have shown in making their own hard-won information freely available to me, and in tracing local people with memories. Whatever help has been given, however, I remain responsible for any errors. I have tried to be sure that I have acknowledged the source of every photograph or postcard not deposited in a public collection or belonging to me. In some cases, people lending me material may not have been aware of any copyright holders, so I have no means of knowing whether any rights are held by anyone. Where a name was indicated on an image, I have made every effort to try and trace it. If I have failed to acknowledge anyone in this book, I apologise here and now.

In the following list of sources, the numbers refer to the pages, 'u' means upper, and 'l' means lower. Acocks Green Junior School: 95l, 96u, 96l; John Alder via Mike Wood: 71u; Birmingham City Council Department of Planning and Architecture: 29l, 30l, 32u, 33l, 35u, 35l, 37u, 40u, 109l; Val Blick: 53u, 73l; John Bick: 31l, 39l, 42u, 42l, 50l, 58u, 107, 112u, 112l; Mike Clarke: 14l (Mike Wood), 32l (Mike Wood), 54u, 71l (W.N. Dixon); Charles Coldrick: 83; Joan Cooper via Mary Smith: 128l; Andrew Coulles: 72u, 72l; Marjorie Davies via Mary Smith: 18l, 19u, 19l, 81, 82u; Rosemary Eade via Mary Smith: 77l; John Gilbert: 80u, 80l; Margaret Glass: 16u; Josephine Gloster: 90u; Rick Green: 49 (E.W. Hannon), 52u, 54l, 55u; Betty Harrison: 46l; Hay Mills Fire Station: 79l; Holy Souls Church: 92u, 119l; Ethel Hone: 75u; Kath Huckfield: 92l; the late Eric Ivison: 46u; John Russell Izod: 12, 13u, 84; D.K. Jones via Mike Wood: 52; Joan Jones: 50u; Dianne Kenny and Margarette Woodruff: 28l, 67u, 67l, 85u, 85l, 86u, 86l, 87u, 125u; Travel West Midlands/Kithead Trust (Derek Potter): 63u, 63l; Connie Maund: 21u, 87l, 88u, 97u, 121u; Estella McAllister: 98u; Midlands Co-operative Society (Sue Letts): 74u, 75l, 76u, 76l, 77u; Patrick Moynihan: 105l, 106; H.B. Oliver via Mary Smith: 93; Olive Palser: 104u, 126u; Jean Pearce: 68u, 68l; Revd Richard Postill: 14u, 47u, 90l, 91u, 91l, 114u, 115l, 117u; Ron Powell: 105u, 127u; Dorothy Rabouhans: 102l, 103u; Mary Seaton: 99u, 100u, 100l, 101u; Mary Smith: 43u, 69l, 79u, 89u, 89l, 98l, 101l, 104l, 126l; Karl Thomas: 11u, 11l, 18u, 22u, 23l, 33u, 34u, 41u, 48u, 78u, 108u, 116u, 120u, 120l, 125l; Nancy Turner via Mary Smith: 37l, 38u; Frank Wells: 29u, 51, 58l, 66u, 66l, 70u, 70l, 88l, 114l, 124l, 127l, 128u; Ava Westwood: 94u, 94l, 95u, 127l; Maurice White: 16l, 113l, Peter White: 43l, 65, 111u, 118, 119u, 124u; Eric Williamson: 53l, 116l; Geoff Wood via Mike Wood: 30u; Mike Wood: 31u, 64u; Valerie Worthing: 97l.

Introduction

Acocks Green is one of Birmingham's most important and historic suburbs and many fine old houses still remain from its Victorian heyday. During this century it became one of the best shopping centres in the whole city. The story of its development through the years of Victorian sophistication and its twentieth century transformation into Birmingham 27 is told in this book alongside photographs dating from the turn of the century until 1965.

Acocks Green was a part of the ancient Parish of Yardley, which stretched for seven and a half miles from Yardley Wood to Lea Village. The area around today's centre was not the first settlement, though. This was further north, near Mansfield Road. In 1275 it was called Tenelee, which means 'the clearing of ten fields'. Later called Tenchlee, it had a higher population than Yardley village itself in the early fourteenth century. Its centre might have been a green, or a stockfield, in the triangle between Yardley, Coventry and Stockfield Roads. Tenchlee has completely disappeared as an entity, however. Around and away from the communal fields private enterprise farms and estates appeared, some with moats, like Huyon Hall and Broom Hall. In the fifteenth century, the Fox family bought the farm belonging to the atte Holies. The Acocks acquired Notings land near Woodcock Lane: by 1552 the estate was known as Acockes. Acocks Green House and other estates were given by Richard Acock to his son William as a wedding gift in 1626. This early reference to Acocks Green is therefore to an area on the Warwick Road near the old Spread Eagle and Dolphin inns.

From the late seventeenth century stage coaches stopped at this centre. In 1725 the Warwick Road was turnpiked and a tollgate was placed across the road at the Dolphin, with a weighbridge being installed later. Another transport development came between 1793 and 1799 with the construction of the Birmingham to Warwick canal. Wharves opened at Stockfield and Yardley Road. Tiles, bricks, sand and gravel were exported, and coal and later Welsh slate came in. Increased prosperity brought with it the rebuilding of farms and the construction of large residences, but the real spur to the wealthy moving in came with the opening of the Birmingham to Oxford railway in 1852. Businessmen could leave the dirty and disease-ridden town for a clean and pleasant country life after work or in retirement. I could not conjure up a better picture of Acocks Green at this time than that drawn by Alan Fitton in 1935. 'In those days it would have been difficult to find a more entrancing spot, or one from which the noise and bustle of commerce seemed more remote. A few stately houses, for the most part standing in their own grounds and a number of humbler cottages, picturesque though doubtless insanitary, comprised the homes of the scanty population. [There was] one church - the Congregational. [A few] hostelries were evidence that the villagers were sometimes inclined to wander, but the fact that there were only three trains a day and few other means of transport, ensured that these wanderings should be in a strictly limited area. The roads consisted of winding lanes bounded by hedgerows that were the home of wild flowers and guarded by great trees... Broad stretches of meadow land or fields, farm-tended and fruitful, met the eye on every side. There was no bustle and little noise, unless the song of birds, the murmuring of the stream through the village, and the whistling of a labourer at his work be deemed disturbing.'

At this time there were three separate hamlets along the Warwick Road: Flint Green, Westley Brook, and Acocks Green itself. Mansions now appeared near the railway station, and beautiful houses were built on roads like Botteville Road, Westley Road, and the Warwick Road itself. Soon the centre was being pulled towards the junction of roads at Westley Brook hamlet. The Methodist chapel of 1863, and St Mary's church of 1866 appeared, then the Acocks Green Institute or Public Hall of 1878 was added on Sherbourne Road, providing an astonishing wealth of cultural and social activities. A large number of clubs and societies of all kinds were formed and flourished. A Temperance Institute sought to rival the attractions of the six local pubs: the Spread Eagle, the Dolphin, the Red Lion, the New Inn, the Great Western and the Britannia. However, this middle-class life to rival even an Edgbaston or a Moseley appeared to be threatened by the building of terrace rows on a few streets at the end of the century. *The Birmingham Daily Mail* reported in 1903 that 'wealthy residents who had loved the place for its quiet exclusiveness and pleasant detachment' were 'stealing silently away in the direction of Knowle or Solihull, where the octopus tentacles of expanding Birmingham are as yet in the distance'. Perhaps amongst them were people like those on Yardley Road who forbade the wearing of hobnailed boots while you were walking along the road outside their houses! The exodus continues to this day, of course.

It was the absorption of Yardley into Birmingham in 1911 which caused the greatest change to Acocks Green, however. Trams came to Broad Road from 1916 and to the village from 1922. The city was desperate for land for housing and in a handful of years from 1925 no less than half of Acocks Green was built over with council houses. This kind of low-density housing, with good sanitation and repairs in the rent package, constituted a vital improvement for the less well-off. Some private housing also appeared. Not only was this a drastic change in terms of the loss of farms, fields, country lanes, and so on, it also involved a tremendous social upheaval. Many thousands of people with stronger accents arrived, who appeared to the indigenous population to be socially inferior. Taffy Lewis, author of *Any Road*, recalled on a reminiscence tape made twenty years ago that he used to be ignored in shops until regular customers had been served. 'You were recognised because they did not recognise you'. He felt that many tradesmen were used to and preferred making up orders for the big houses and then delivering them. A man writing to a newspaper in April 1930 lamented: 'There is more fighting, brawling and petty thieving in this once quiet rural suburb than in any other district in Birmingham. Ask any motorist if it is safe to leave a ring or a pair of gloves in a car, and even a milk bottle has been stolen actually out of a child's hand while its mother was in a nearby shop for a few minutes'. Acocks Green was given the name of Snobs Green or Snobs Paradise, and had indeed been known also as Debtors Retreat!

The increase in population brought a great expansion in the number of shops: eventually the total reached two hundred in the whole district. Churches were extended, their sports and social clubs grew and they built meeting rooms and halls. In 1932 the centre of Acocks Green was redesigned. A large island incorporating the tram terminus was created. The 'Green' that we refer to is sixty-five years old, not a remnant of village life and it was without a blade of grass until after the trams left! In fact, as traffic grew and grew, the Green became unreachable across a dangerous sea of vehicles. Shopping changed as well. With the advent of self-service after the war, using shops became a more 'democratic' process. More recently cheap shopping elsewhere, especially in markets and supermarkets, caused the demise of many local family businesses. Some large houses, sports grounds and green spaces have been infilled by higher density housing, and two areas of system-built council housing have recently been demolished and rebuilt. Some of the pubs have also closed.

I hope this book gives pleasure and information to those interested in Acocks Green. I am very grateful to all the individuals who have lent material and also to the Libraries and Learning Division of the city's Department of Leisure and Community Services, which has lent a quarter of the pictures. If anyone else has photographs or postcards that they wish to see made publicly available, the Local Studies and History Department in the Central Library would be pleased to hear from them on 0121-303-4549.

One

Rural Views

Gospel House Farm, Gospel Lane, 1912. This beautiful scene was captured for the sale of the Severne family's Hall Green Estate in 1912. There was a large oak nearby on the parish boundary called the Gospel Oak, which was felled in the 1840s. Sixteen horses were needed to drag it away. The King family tenanted the farm for several generations.

Gospel Farm, c. 1920. The city compulsorily purchased the ninety-two acre farm from E.C.W. Severne and Mrs R.I. Wynn. No agreement could be reached on price and it had to go to arbitration: the sale went through on 3 May 1929 for £12,900.

A bomb crater in a field belonging to Gospel Farm, April 1918. Hauptmann Kuno Manger's Zeppelin L62 made an attack on Birmingham on 12 April, but he turned back in the face of a barrage of anti-aircraft fire before reaching the centre of the city and dropped a 300kg bomb here. (Thanks to Joe McKenna for this information.)

Beech Lane, i.e. Gospel Lane, c. 1905.

A leisurely outing picking fruit on the lane, c. 1905. Gospel Lane was known as Langley Lane in 1609. For a few years this century it was still known as Beech Lane, or Beeches Lane. The Beech family were at Redstone Farm at the Warwick Road end. Another local name was Walls Lane, after another farming family there. Rather curiously, Redstone Farm gave its name to the southern end of the road when the council estates were built, some say to distinguish the Hall Green end from the more common Acocks Green stretch!

Broomhall Farm, a painting of unknown date. No doubt this vision of pastoral bliss is not exactly true to life, but who cares? This lovely picture is in the possession of John Russell Izod, grandson of the last farmer at Broomhall. Broomhall is one of the oldest names in the area, mentioned as early as 972 in the name Bromhalas, meaning shallow valleys where broom grows. The de Bromhales were important landowners here in their moated hall. Their wealth survived the Black Death and the Great Famine, but the estate was divided up in the fifteenth century due to the lack of a male heir. However, Broomhall was still such an important entity in Tudor times that it gave its name to no less than half of Yardley Parish. Later the name applied just to the area between the Stratford and Warwick Roads. This administrative division was known as Broomhall Quarter. The estate was in the hands of the King family by 1836.

Broomhall Farm, c. 1925. The Izod family moved here c. 1921 from Hall Green Hall Farm and stayed until 1947. Joseph Wheildon Izod's wife Fanny Sophia was born a King. (See page 84 for more information.)

The dam on the millstream, Fox Hollies Park, April 1936. Lt.-Col. Zaccheus Walker had his stud farm here at Sandpits Farm. The park area is historically important: it has Bronze Age burnt mounds, which were possibly saunas or industrial sites, the site of Broomhall Mill and the fishpond from Pool Farm. It took years of levelling, draining and planting to make the park: what a pity it is that vandalism and anti-social behaviour prevent local people enjoying it to the full today.

Dolphin Lane, c. 1905. Another contemporary postcard view, very similar, is titled Shady Lane. Until the mid-1920s the official name was Green Lane. The Dolphin pub was at the Warwick Road end of the lane. This scene is quite magical.

Another view of Dolphin Lane, c. 1920. The building is part of Pool Farm, which stood on a bend in the lane. The bend was removed when the houses were built, and the lane was extended to a point further down Shirley Road.

Hyron Hall Farm, c. 1925. Hyron Hall was another local moated site. The farm was demolished in 1928. Starcross Road runs between the site of the farm buildings and the remnant of the moat, just cutting into one end of it. Connie Maund recalls getting milk in a jug from here and going fishing in the pool at Victoria Road as a child, when she lived at Ivycots on Hazelwood Road.

The stable yard at Hyron Hall Farm, c. 1925.

Stooks in the field opposite 98 Greenwood Road, c. 1925. Northanger Road was built here. Mrs Margaret Glass used to visit her grandparents Ernest Edwin and Florence Wykes here, who had a dog called Jimmy. She told me that her grandmother used to attach a message to Jimmy's collar and send him across the fields and along the Ninestiles Path (the York Road section) to 33 Russell Road, Hall Green, where Margaret's aunt Marjorie Young lived! The dog would return with the reply. Greenwood Road became Olton Boulevard East c. 1928 and the name was transferred to the extravagant showpiece Avenue nearby, to which coachloads of visitors were brought in order to admire municipal estate planning. (See also page 48.)

Shirley Road, 1920. This was built up for only a short distance from the village, then became a very narrow lane with high holly hedges. It was widened in 1931/2.

Fox Hollies Hall, c. 1910. This Italianate rebuild dated from 1869/70 and was commissioned by Zaccheus Walker III, a retired merchant. According to the directory, he was at Hyron Hall in 1868. When his health began to fail his son Zaccheus IV returned from his profession as a draughtsman and engineer at the age of thirty-two to run the estate. This was c. 1880. Zaccheus IV had a long career in the Volunteer Reserve, whence he got his rank of Lt.-Col. He was also Vice-Chairman of Yardley District Council and played an important role on many other Boards and Committees. He was a noted breeder of horses and mastiffs. Local people remember him as the unofficial squire of Acocks Green. As late as 1912 he bought land close to the Hall. On 7 April 1925 he sold the Dolphin pub to Mitchells and Butlers for £5,000. On 27 April 1925 he sold the three-acre triangle of land between Summer, Fox Hollies and (then) Spring Road to M & B for £5,745 (see page 18) and then sold off two hundred and sixty-two acres to the city on 26 May 1925 for £34,001. His home was soon surrounded by houses, shops and the Fox Hollies pub. Altogether, over 2,500 council houses were built on the land, which stretched as far as Broomhall. The Fox Hollies Hall Estate development was seen as a high-water mark in municipal design, with variations in house frontages, tiles and slate roofs, stucco and brick facades, together forming at least twenty different designs on gracefully curving roads. The private grounds that Lt.-Col. Walker retained for his lifetime as part of the sale were seen by local lads as a challenge. The late Eric Ivison told me he used to go scrumping for apples in the grounds of the Hall and had to run for his life at the sound or sight of the large dogs that were kept there! Things were not always so. Zaccheus Walker used to throw his grounds open for various good purposes and on Saturday 12 September 1896 he hosted an outing for over seven hundred children from All Saints, one of the poorest parts of Birmingham. They were brought by special train to enjoy a day out in the country, with games and food arranged. Lt.-Col. Walker died on 5 December 1930 at the age of 82. Les Smith recalled coming out of Hartfield Crescent school at lunchtime and seeing the funeral procession, which included a gun carriage with the Union Jack draped over the coffin. (See pages 18 and 82 for more information). Lt.- Col. Walker is buried in the family vault at St. Mary's, Handsworth.

Fox Hollies Road at the Hall gates on a card posted on 11 July 1908. A pair of restored gates and posts stands today near the bus stop. The Hall was taken down by 1937. Zaccheus Walker did not live to see the widening of Fox Hollies Road in front of his home during the first part of 1931 and Greenwood Avenue had only been cut as far as where the eventual dual carriageway would run past, so he enjoyed the benefit of the high hedges all his life, even if he had to put up with trespass and other nuisances. Tower blocks with names recalling the estate were built by 1965 on part of what later became a public park many years after its 1937 transfer to the parks committee

Foxes Green, c. 1905 on a card posted on 13 October 1917. The cottage was occupied by Lt.-Col. Walker's kennelmaster, Joseph Smith (see pages 19, 47, 81 and 82). The Fox Hollies pub was opened here in 1928 (see page 110).

Sir Kenneth, a prizewinner for Lt.-Col. Walker, c. 1909.

Part of the kennels, Fox Hollies Hall, c. 1910. This spaniel, named Bruce, belonged to Joseph Smith.

High hedges at Fox Hollies Road, 18 March 1931. This was photographed by the Public Works Department just before the road was widened.

Shaftmoor Lane in winter, c. 1900.

A leisurely stroll at the Vineries bridge, c. 1905. The late Victorian house is just visible through the trees. Its large garage was underneath the house. The Vineries was where a large market garden business was operating by 1905. Around 1922 it was bought by the Westwood family, who were well-known fruiterers. They sold the estate in 1936, after receiving an offer from a government agency. The Rover 'shadow' factory began making aircraft parts there in July 1937.

The wind-powered water pump at the Vineries, 1933. The water was stored in a large open tank. Tomatoes and chrysanthemums were grown in the greenhouses and frames and vegetables in the open ground. There were also poultry sheds, a pigeon loft, fruit trees and a rose garden, a bowling green and a small pavilion. Joseph Westwood built modern sheds there for his favourite Gloucester Old Spot pigs, for which he won prizes. The house was not knocked down when the factory was built, and was later bought by the Co-op. Stables housed the laundry's horses, and the laundry boilerman lived in the house. From c. 1969 it was rented by Acocks Green Demolition, who bought it a couple of years later. They had a plant hire business on the site until a few years ago. (Thanks to Charles Coldrick and Bill Law for this information: see also page 83.)

Woodcock Lane, c. 1905 on a card posted on 31 December 1920. The lane was cut through by the Avenue in the 1890s. Woodberry Walk is on part of the old line of the lane from the Warwick Road to the railway: it was also known as Muddy Lane. The new Woodcock Lane further down the Warwick Road was made in the late 1950s.

Quality Lane, c. 1890. This is now Arden Road. Two of the old cottages may be seventeenth century and are the oldest survivals in Acocks Green. The water pump in one of the gardens worked until the railway embankment was cut and interrupted the water supply. The tree survives on an island in the middle of the road.

Cottages at Flint Green Road, 25 April 1937. These attractive timber-framed buildings were demolished c. 1952.

Stockfield Road at the Warwick Road, c. 1905. On the left is the Congregational church, and in the centre is the extremely narrow bridge over the railway. The road used to be called Rushall Lane. (See pages 55-7 and 121.)

Stockfield Farm, 29 July 1925. The farm stood where the Warwick Road-bound carriageway runs just south of Kilmorie Road.

The canal bridge at Stockfield Road, 29 July 1925. Over the next year the bridge was replaced by a wider bridge on a dual carriageway. Next to the lamp post is a fire alarm point, an important facility before telephones were common in homes.

Two

Suburban Scenes

The corner of Fox Hollies Road and Westley Road, 18 March 1931. The Recreation Ground was formerly called Heath Croft and was given to Yardley District Council by the Yardley Charity Estates in 1898. It was formally opened in 1902 to celebrate the Coronation. A fire call point is at the corner. Fox Green Farm and its fields were to the right: the farmhouse survives as a yoga school.

Westley Road, c. 1905, on a card posted on 12 August 1909. It was known as Well Lane in 1872 and also later as Florence Road. A publicity booklet for the 1926 Outer Circle route described the road as 'an old-fashioned lane...[with]...open country on the right...'

Westley Road at the Green, March 1931. The old New Inn, as it were, which dates from 1873 at the latest, is on the right and the tram terminus at Ivy Cottage is on the left.

The farm buildings at Ivy Cottage, c. 1931. This site was compulsorily purchased in January 1931 and the library was built there, opening on 14 June 1932. The extent of the ivy growth can be seen: it even came in through the windows! When the builders tried to demolish this timber-framed cottage the steel hawsers broke and it had to be pulled down bit-by-bit. Local people still remember Miss Elizabeth Mary Ann Attewell Orsborn, who lived there and who used to ride her horse, Prince, side-saddle. She moved to 41 Dudley Park Road in 1931 and died in Autumn 1935.

Looking up Shirley Road from the Green, 13 April 1931.

The Green after alterations, 10 October 1932. The New Inn opened on 2 March 1932. Shops and a bank were built on the opposite side of Westley Road by 1934.

The Green from the opposite side, c. 1933. This postcard was lent to me by Dianne Kenny, daughter of Fred Cowan Junior. Fred's Cafe and the family car are marked on the card. Brooke Oliver told me people used to say they were going down to the 'C'-front here: Clissold, Cowan, Clewer, Collier, Cuttriss and Cooper were in the row! (See also pages 67 and 85-7.)

The row from Dudley Park Road to the Green, c. 1902. The wall at a double row of cottages, Westley Brook Cottages, is on the right before the New Inn. A coalman is visiting one of the buildings on the left, which are at this time a private house, the post office, a cycle manufacturer, and Martins the pork butchers. The area in front of the new Metropolitan Bank building and the three cottages in the distance is a triangular 'green'. According to V.J. Tustin it was actually a garden owned by a cab proprietor, who lived in the first cottage and hung his washing out there! That block was replaced by Burtons and Woolworths in the mid-1930s.

The same row, photographed on 6 September 1951.

The Green in 1965. The post office had been enlarged and modernised in 1935. The lack of vehicles and the ability to park here astounds the modern eye. (See page 65 for more on the earlier post office.)

The next few shops on the Warwick Road, 18 March 1955. The entire row was replaced between March 1973 and 1976. The new red brick shop row is set further back. The alterations made flooding from the village stream, the Westley Brook, even worse. The late Eric Ivison told me that on one occasion floodwater pushed over a wall in the telephone exchange in Station Road and Mason Bros, where he worked, was under two feet of water. The Green itself also used to flood. The main sewer near here was enlarged in 1989.

The Green at the corner of Shirley Road, c. 1900. The house on the right belonged to Clifford the butcher, and was next to his premises. He owned the fields at the back, where he kept cattle. There was also a slaughterhouse at the back of his shop.

The Green at the corner of Shirley Road, c. 1910.

The shop row from the Midland Bank, 9 September 1958. The bank premises were built in 1901 to be a clothing factory, but the Metropolitan Bank of England and Wales moved in there from across the road. It was amalgamated with the Midland Bank in 1914. The chambers above have been used by a variety of businesses. Pitts lived above their shop: it is just possible to see where the shop used to be because the newer bricks are a slightly different shade of pink (see also page 69).

Looking back to the Green, c. 1904. A.J. Walker manufactured cycles, and was only a few doors away from another manufacturer, Henry Thomas Law, who was near the post office (see page 29).

Station Road, c. 1905. Deeds lent to me by Mrs Wilcox of Dudley Park Road show that this used to be known as Purrott Road. William Henry Bailey, hairdresser; Francis Meteyard, bootmaker; and Thomas Simmons, blacksmith are shown here.

Station Road, February 1956.

The Warwick Road near Station Road, c. 1901 on a card posted on 1 August 1905. The postcard was produced by George Lewis, stationer, seen here. To the left of his business is H. Chappell, saddler and harness maker. To the right are William Hodges, coffee house; John Garbett and Co., grocers and Edwin Stubbs, chemist and druggist. At the far corner of Station Road is the building remodelled to be the Picture Playhouse in 1913. Deborah Bridges, grocer and Samuel Bridges, builder are listed there in 1901.

The Warwick Road at Station Road, 12 June 1934. Milk is being delivered by cycle, with the churns being carried in the wooden 'sidecar'. Keight and Soden used to deliver by two-wheeled light gig pulled by a high-stepping horse, as did other butchers. The gig would call on wealthy customers for their order and deliver it in time to be cooked for the next meal.

A similar view, 6 January 1961. Paynes the shoe repairers are in the building which stands on the foundations of the Picture Playhouse. They were in business there from c. 1943.

The next few shops, 7 July 1953.

This is how the row finished on 21 May 1936. A short block of shops has replaced Eastbourne House (see pages 105-6). The road will be widened at the gardens on the left (see page 38).

Looking back from the Red Lion to Station Road, 12 June 1934. Note the horse trough outside the pub. Older photographs show a lower trough in front for dogs and a handpump.

The Warwick Road, 11 August 1950. The newer block of shops is on the right. Halfords had a large workshop at the back, according to Mike Wood.

Clearing the land for self-build houses at Mallard Close, 1964. These were built between 1964 and 1967 by the Octave Group on a former bowling green. Holy Souls R.C. primary school, which opened a decade later, stands in the grounds and on the site of the Grove, formerly an architect's house. The new Co-op row opened in 1962, replacing most of an orchard. Mallard Close follows its right-hand edge.

Construction at Mallard Close, c. 1965. Nancy Turner lent these photographs. Tragically, her husband was killed before their house was finished and the others finished it for her, as was the agreement.

The Warwick Road beyond the Red Lion, 31 May 1939. Widening here was completed by August 1938. Dr Dain ran a practice from George Perkins' house on the left. The shop row at 1160 Warwick Road opened c. 1960, with flats above, and stretches from the older shops at Oxford Road back to the house site, covering Dr Allen's surgery as well. The wall on the right survives in Sainsbury's car park: it used to be the convent school/Crosby Hall wall (see pages 93-5). An older boundary wall further out can be seen in the central reservation.

The Warwick Road after widening from Victoria Road, 25 May 1936. This work was finally approved in June 1935. Matthew Bissell, the publican at the Spread Eagle for four decades, went to the Fox Hollies for a few years, but returned to occupy premises right behind his old haunts when the shops were built, opening the confectioners seen on the right. He was there from c. 1932 to c. 1939.

The shops at the corner of Oxford Road, c. 1907. In 1888, Oxford Road was the name for Sherbourne Road, and from c. 1900 until c. 1905, the part of Oxford Road from here to Roberts Road was known as Clifton Road. The style of the upper stories of these shops suits the way the ground floor is presented and today's shop fronts look incongruous here: they suit the newer shops nearer the Green much better.

The Warwick Road from Oxford Road, 20 October 1952. For more on Dennett and Coulles see page 72. Logan-Dixon is one of Wilfred Norman Dixon's shops (see page 71).

The Warwick Road looking back from beyond the Dolphin, 12 October 1932. This was the first part to be widened. The old Dolphin and the Spread Eagle stood where the left-hand carriageway is here. (See the section on Social Life for more on the pubs. For more on Alder's Garage see page 71.)

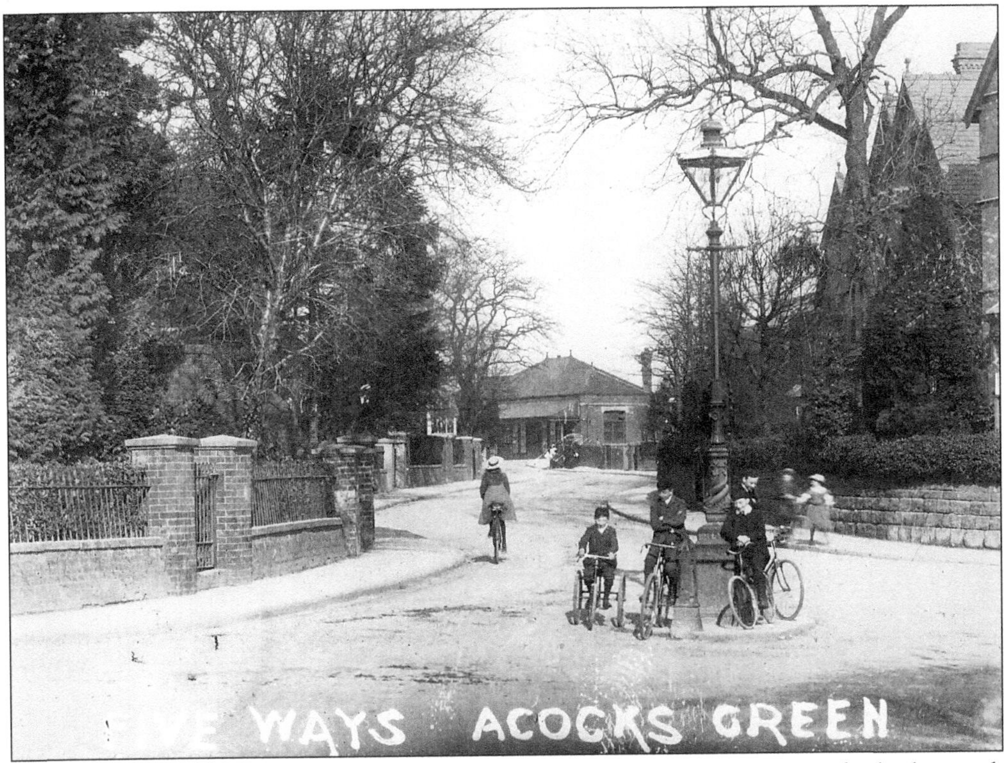

Five Ways, Acocks Green on a card posted on 9 July 1909. The station is in the background. This local Five Ways is a life-threatening junction nowadays, even for motorists. How times have changed!

Walking down Sherbourne Road in one's best clothes, c. 1910. Perhaps these people are on their way to St Mary's church. The Stationmaster's house is behind the tree.

The Market Place, Yardley Road, c. 1907 on a card posted on 29 August 1923. Until some time after the War, Yardley Road was an excellent shopping centre. Mike and Ann Clarke told me they had little need to go down to the village to shop when they first lived on Malvern Road in the 1960s.

Yardley Road Parade, c. 1910. The shops are at Douglas Road. Ladies are off on a cycle ride, perhaps into the countryside of Yardley and Sheldon.

Bomb damage at Cottesbrook Road, Friday 16 August 1940. This was only the third air raid on Birmingham and this and the house opposite were destroyed in the small hours. Two people were killed. At the time, the raid was seen as a novelty by some: apparently people came on the Outer Circle bus to stare from the end of the road.

The Warwick Road at Broad Road on a card posted on 26 November 1910. The 1871 vicarage and St Mary's can be seen on the left.

The Warwick Road at the corner of Stockfield Road, 25 April 1937. On the left is the smithy (see page 78). The lamp belonging to the Britannia Inn is visible beyond (see page 111). The small garage on the right, run by J.W. Gethin, eventually took over the whole row, including the gabled house known as Tyseley Grange. Colliers also expanded round the corner into Stockfield Road. They gave up their well-known garage at the Swan in 1980. The Grange Social Club had to make a hasty move to Broad Road from Tyseley Grange when the extension to the premises were announced, according to George Slack.

Stockfield Road at Douglas Road, 29 July 1925. This will shortly be part of a municipal estate. The building on the left is a shop run by James Eades. Behind the hedge stood Stockfield House.

Stockfield Road near the canal bridge, 5 February 1925. William T. Rabone sold Stockfield House and nearly twenty-one acres of land to the city on 20 November 1923 for £4,300. William Mansfield and others sold over seven acres fronting Wynford Road on 4 August 1927 for £1,447. The other purchase which made up the Stockfield Estate was on the other side of Stockfield Road: six acres from the Governors of Yardley Educational Foundation on 13 June 1924 for £3,400. This last piece is no longer to be used for housing. At the time this picture was taken, the Parkinson-Kahn system-built houses which made up the estate were being built. They included pre-cast reinforced concrete panels. Unfortunately, the mix contained sulphates and chlorides, which later attacked the concrete. Half of the houses had been sold under the right-to-buy legislation of 1980 by the time they were designated as defective and not repairable within grant limits, under the Housing Defects Act of 1984. They were bought back and demolished from 1989-1995 and have been replaced by an award-winning redevelopment guided by the Stockfield Community Association. This is a company composed of residents, Bromford Carinthia Housing Association and the Halifax Building Society. Houses are for rent, shared ownership and private ownership arranged with cul-de-sacs rather than through routes and with traffic calming included. The new buildings were commended in 1994 in the Birmingham Design Awards. The assessors were impressed by the new housing layout, which carefully integrated the buildings into existing avenues of mature trees, thereby recreating community living in an environment of improved quality. Thanks to Tony Roberts and Kevan Harrison for help with this information.

Yarnfield Road, c. 1927. The view is from Wardle Grove towards Mayfield Road. Trees were planted and pavements were provided in the same year. This municipal estate is made up of three smaller purchases between June 1923 and January 1925 and the Tyseley Farm Estate of 79 acres, bought on 21 December 1926. The city paid £24,250 overall.

Spring Road on a card posted on 3 January 1913 by Ernest Seal to his future wife (thanks to Betty Harrison for this card). The house which juts out into the road was a doctors' surgery until Lucas built a new entrance there. Spring Road was called Lydestree Laine in 1562, and used to run through to Fox Hollies Road until the pub and shops were built, when the last stretch was renamed.

Summer Road on a card posted on 25 January 1911. Joseph Smith lived in the cottage on the right (see page 18).

Hazelwood Road, 13 April 1931. Since then this most attractive tree-lined scene has undergone many changes. No. 63 on the left was destroyed by bombing in 1940. To its left is the Methodist Tennis and Bowling Club (c. 1920-1968). Green Acres was built on the club site around 1969 and three houses (nos 63-67) replaced the original no. 63. The large house on the right (no. 58) was replaced by Hazelwood Court around 1970. No. 62 was replaced by three houses around 1980 and the grounds became garages for Coppice Drive. Just beyond Hazelwood Court is Dogge Lane Croft, recalling the name for Hazelwood Road in 1580. This is an infill development from around 1987, which involved the removal of no. 56. Beyond there is another club, the Hazelwood Lawn Tennis and Bowling Club (c. 1923-1965), which together with nos 24-26 and Jones' Nursery (c. 1943-1963) in Shirley Road, were replaced by Hazeltree Croft in 1965. See also page 49.

Greenwood Road, c. 1905. The road has become part of Olton Boulevard East, and most of it is lined with municipal houses. On page 16 is a view over the right-hand side of this road, taken from one of these houses.

Municipal housing on Olton Boulevard East, c. 1928. The laundry van belongs to the Victoria and Yardley Laundry, Church Road, Yardley.

Three

Transport

A horse at Acocks Green, c. 1898. The bus route is from High Street via Sparkbrook and Tyseley to Acocks Green, and the operator is the Birmingham General Omnibus Company. They bought out Charles Lane, who had been a horse bus operator for some years, but went into liquidation themselves in 1899. Charles Lane become a very rich man through landownership and his transport activities. The advertisement on the bus is for Walter B. Child, FRHS, the great hardy plant specialist and garden contractor of Acocks Green. According to the directories, he had a nursery at Shamrock Cottage, Greenwood Road, until 1897, when he moved to Hazelwood Road. His house Edelweiss, was on Westley Road across from the school. Walter Child stayed at Hazelwood Road until 1906, when Charles Henry Herbert took over. Child was listed as a nurseryman at Edelweiss until 1910, when he moved over to the school side of Westley Road (Poplar Cottages). He ran his business from there until the end of the first World War. Charles Herbert was in charge at Hazelwood Road until around 1933, after which others ran the business until its replacement by flats.

A horse bus from High Street to Acocks Green and other horse-drawn transport at the Spread Eagle, c. 1900. Horse buses served Acocks Green from the 1860s.

Acocks Green Railway Station, 1905. This was the year before the station was rebuilt. Construction of the line involved excavation of a mile-long cutting over thirty feet deep. The first station had a couple of sheds, a man porter, a lad porter, two signalmen and a stationmaster. The signalman on duty had to walk up and down the line to operate the signals by hand until c. 1880, when block signals were introduced.

Commuters wait at the newly rebuilt Acocks Green Station, c. 1907. The station is on the Birmingham to Oxford line, opened on 1 October 1852 for passengers and in February 1853 for goods. It had been planned by the Birmingham and Oxford Junction Railway, but the Great Western took over the line and built it to mixed gauge. This involved laying three rails, the third one being able to take the Broad Gauge vehicles favoured by Isambard Kingdom Brunel, the GWR's chief engineer. The broad gauge was seven feet, and the 'narrow' gauge four feet eight and a half inches. Brunel lost the Battle of the Gauges, however. This stretch of line was reduced to the narrower gauge by April 1869. The station was renamed Acocks Green and South Yardley in October 1878. Tyseley station was built in 1906 as the junction station for the new North Warwickshire Line. In that year the line through Acocks Green was quadrupled as far as Olton and the station was rebuilt. Bryan Holden wrote in 1984 of a letter he had received from Harry Margetts. A signalman at the station during the war, Mr Margetts used to call out 'all clear' through a megaphone to the people in shelters near the line: he got the news early through being in direct communication with Snow Hill. Later, Harry Margetts became stationmaster at Acocks Green and Olton from 1953 until 1964. In the 1950s Acocks Green station had seven staff: a stationmaster, senior and junior porters, senior and junior booking clerks, a parcels clerk and a lamp man (thanks to Eric Williamson for this information). The great days of steam gave way to diesel traction in the 1960s, to the distress of countless enthusiasts, and the station buildings here were taken down in one week from 27 March 1968. The footbridge at the Roberts Road end was also removed along with the two relief lines. Lower maintenance costs were the justification, plus the need for car parking. There also used to be a goods loop at Acocks Green until then, and Bryan Holden, looking back to the 1940s, recalled in 1980 in the Evening Mail that pigs used be kept overnight in trucks there, causing local residents to keep their windows tightly shut! Mike Clarke remembers passenger coaches, some from other parts of the railway network, being kept on the loop line at Bank Holidays, ready for use at Snow Hill and New Street.

GWR engine 617 at Acocks Green in 1912. This engine was a 2-4-0 'Metropolitan' tank built in 1871. This type of engine was built for suburban traffic and acquired the nickname as it was often used to run over the Metropolitan Railway from the GWR. In October 1930 this particular engine was fitted for auto-train working. This was one of several designs the GWR developed for economical working, like steam railmotors and diesel railcars (see pages 54-5). Auto-trains often had only one carriage. In an auto-train the driver worked from the engine in one direction, but from a compartment in the carriage in the other direction. The fireman remained on the footplate: various means of communication between them were used. Rick Green tells me that on some occasions on branch lines, or where Inspectors were not about, the control cables to the brakes and regulator from the driver's compartment in the carriage were disconnected, allowing the fireman to drive, while he leaned out of the engine to check the line! (Thanks to Mike Wood for obtaining this picture from the D.K. Jones Collection.)

Acocks Green station in happy times during the early 1950s, winning a prize as best-kept station, under stationmaster Alfred Compton (see also page 73).

An A1A-A1A diesel electric loco passing through Acocks Green, February 1954. Eric Williamson took this photograph of an engine made for the Commonwealth Railway in Australia. It was on a test run, apparently loaded with sandbags to simulate the weight of passengers.

A rather dirty engine with passenger coaches at Acocks Green, photographed by Mike Clarke in 1962. The goods loop is on the left, with the four lines, two main and two relief, shown. This is a 7000 Series Castle Class locomotive, number 7008 Swansea Castle.

A GWR 0-4-2 tank engine number 847 on a Stratford local train at Spring Road on the North Warwickshire Line, c. 1928. The line opened for goods on 9 December 1907 and for passengers on 1 July 1908. Spring Road was called a 'platform'. This was where a full-length train could stop, but where full station facilities were not provided. Apart from normal trains, steam railmotors, carriages with a small steam engine in a compartment at one end, worked this line in the early days.

A 'Flying Banana' at Spring Road, c. 1939. Two types of streamlined diesel railcar could be seen on this line. No. 5 was one of a set of three (nos 5-7) used on local and suburban services, here to Henley-in-Arden. It had sixty-eight seats. It entered service on 22 July 1935 and was withdrawn in December 1957. The horns were added by 1938 to improve safety for railway workers, who could not hear the railcars coming from far enough away. The other type, nos 2-4, was used on the first diesel express passenger service in the country, which began on 9 July 1934 between Birmingham and Cardiff. These railcars had lavatories, a buffet compartment and removable tables between the seats. They could take forty passengers. Both types used 130bhp modified London bus engines capable of a top speed of 75-80mph. The engines were made by AEC and the bodywork by the Gloucester Carriage and Wagon Company. The express service was withdrawn at the outbreak of war, but reinstated in a limited way early in 1940. Late in 1941, the buffet cars were replaced by larger twin units, which could take an additional coach in the middle. Thanks to Mike Wood for help with this information.

The old railway bridge at Stockfield Road, 27 September 1937. Rushey Lane leads off to the left over the bridge.

Stockfield Road bridge, 23 March 1939. It was replaced by a wider bridge between 1939 and 1940.

A train passing under the bridge, 11 July 1939. Visible between the tracks is the ramp for Automatic Train Control. This was a GWR innovation, first developed around 1910, and later refined and improved. It gave an audible warning to the driver if the next signal was not clear and the brakes started to be applied. If he did not respond, the brakes would be fully applied automatically.

A view of the new bridge and the completed road works, 18 March 1941. Stockfield Hall on the right had been compulsorily purchased by the city for road widening on 29 September 1924 for £2,000. It was not needed for that purpose and the city accepted an offer from the War Office in 1929 for it to be used by the 143rd Field Ambulance Corps of the Territorial Army. They marched there on Saturday 6 June 1931 to open it formally. Stockfield Hall survived until the late 1960s.

The canal at Acocks Green on a card posted in December 1907. It was built as the Birmingham to Warwick Canal. Construction began in 1793 and involved at Acocks Green the excavation by pick and shovel of a huge cutting. The canal opened in 1799. At Stockfield there were wharves for transporting bricks and tiles, at Yardley Road sand and gravel were extracted and exported and coal was imported from the Black Country and Staffordshire (see pages 76 and 77).

The canal at Acocks Green on a card posted on 15 July 1915.

The canal bridge at the Vineries, c. 1910. This is the only original bridge to survive. The city planned to replace it with a wider bridge carrying a widened Woodcock Lane, while they were building the Avenue municipal estate, but this plan was not carried out. The bridge has now been listed.

The approach to the old canal bridge at Lincoln Road, 22 June 1934. There was a nasty turn as you came to this humped bridge, and many vehicles either tried to drive too fast and crashed, or came to a halt on the bridge, rocking on their large flywheels, according to Tom Morris. They had to be pushed off the hump to get them on the move again!

The old Lincoln Road bridge from the canal, 22 June 1934.

The new Lincoln Road canal bridge, 11 October 1935.

The old Stockfield Road canal bridge, August 1923. It was replaced in 1925-1926.

A tram at the terminus at Ivy Cottage, 3 May 1923. When the tram track was first constructed, it was laid as a single track between Broad Road and the Green. The road could not be widened at the church and graveyard, where vehicles also had to be allowed to stand, and widening on the other side would have meant dangerously steep carriage drives for the residents. The line had been authorised in 1912 in connection with road widening, and one person, who opposed trams along the road, made an objection that the authorisation had not been complied with as the road was unaltered. This legal challenge prevented the trams running to the village for six years: they started on 2 February 1916 but ran only as far as Broad Road. The city could only get around the problem by inserting a clause in the 1922 Birmingham Corporation Act which said that this tramline should be treated as if it had been constructed in accordance with the Tramways Act of 1912. At the hearing before the Local Legislation Committee on 10 April 1922, the city had to negotiate with the Board of Trade as well, because there was not a distance of nine feet six inches between the outside of a tram and the pavement. Whatever happened, this width could not be achieved on both sides without road widening, but the representative from the Board let the city's proposal through that they should make one pavement narrower to the minimum of six feet to achieve the carriageway width on that side only. Some wide vehicles would have to pass on the wrong side of the road, but there were precedents elsewhere in the city. The original objector was silent in 1922: perhaps he had realised that a lot of people were being inconvenienced by having to walk the distance to and from Broad Road, and that a tram parked at Broad Road was more of a nuisance than one in the village centre. Thus the clause went through, and trams ran to the position here from 9 October 1922.

A tram on the single track stretch of line between the Green and Broad Road, 8 January 1935.

The new tram terminus, 10 October 1932. When the Green was enlarged, this tram terminus with shelter was made in the middle of the new island. The tracks had to be slightly realigned (see page 70). However, motor buses, and especially cheaper diesel buses, were beginning to win the day because of their route flexibility. Acocks Green never saw trolleybuses and the trams finished on 5 January 1937. Later that year, residents suggested that the now empty island should be planted up.

The new Acocks Green Bus Garage, July 1928. The garage opened on 19 June 1928 to cater for the southern half of the Outer Circle route and for the new routes that were being developed in this part of the city.

Buses on Fox Hollies Road, 6 February 1942. The Hockley depot had been bombed on 22/23 November 1940 and many buses were destroyed. A policy of overnight dispersal from local garages followed. Here the bus engines are being kept frost-free by immersion heaters powered from lamp posts. The arrow drawn on the photograph indicates the leads going to plugs on the nearside of the chassis frame. The muffs are keeping the radiators cosy.

A bus accident near Oxford Road, c. 1955. It is amazing how the bus got so near to the shops and failed to hit them. The small boy in the middle left of the picture is Mike Wood, who provided this and several other photographs for this book.

An Outer Circle bus at Yardley Road, 13 June 1934. It is trying to negotiate the awkward bend by the original narrow canal bridge, which was made easier when the bridge was replaced in 1937. The bend is still a problem, however. When approaching from the Swan the road suddenly narrows as you come round it.

Four

Acocks Green at Work

Acocks Green Post Office, c. 1905. It had a blue brick forecourt. Around 1912 it closed and reopened a few doors further into the village a couple of years later, according to the directories. The policeman had a small station a little way behind him: an imposing new station on Yardley Road, which also served as a courthouse, opened in 1909. From c. 1912 a fire station operated from the old police station, with the wheeled escape ladder being kept on the small island triangle at Dudley Park Road. It had been on the corner of Flint Green Road from c. 1899. (See page 79 for more information.)

Alfred Frederick Wells, manager, at Wyman's newspaper stand at Acocks Green station, 1911. He set up on his own later from 22 Florence Road, then bought a round. He always made sure he got the papers from the railway station as early as possible and as his business grew he opened a shop at 1082 Warwick Road on 17 October 1921.

Wells' newsagents, c. 1933. They were postcard publishers as well and remained at this address until 1973, when all the shops on that side from Dudley Park Road to Station Road were demolished. Three years later, the white office tower and the new shops were completed. Alfred's son Frank ran the business from c. 1968. In 1973 he moved to a shop opposite the library on Shirley Road. Sixty years to the day from the opening of the first premises, on 17 October 1981, he retired.

Fred Cowan Senior at his cafe, c. 1932. He moved from Sparkhill to here c. 1920. He died in 1938 and his son Fred Junior carried on with the business. The bus drivers used to bring their billy cans in to the cafe for a refill. In 1977 the premises were rented out to an amusements business, despite local protests. The amuzement arcade also contains the shop next door, which Pearce's sold to them (see page 68).

Girls working in Fred's Cafe, 1950s. The girl with shorter hair is Norma, Fred Junior's sister-in-law, according to Dianne Kenny, his daughter.

Pearce's Fishmongers, Christmas 1936. They opened the shop here c. 1925.

Pearce's after alterations to the shop, Christmas 1938.

Ellard's confectioners, otherwise known as the 'Tuck Shop' for the junior school, 1934. Westley Brook Cottages have already been demolished. Ellard's took over from Mrs Ann Bolton c. 1930: she had been there from c. 1918. Apparently, love letters were left by schoolchildren at 'Old Ma' Bolton's shop!

E. Pitt and Son, Warwick Road by the Midland Bank, c. 1950. They were corn and seed merchants, florists and fruiterers, and sold vegetables, eggs, salad items, and bulbs. They lived over the shop. They were in business here from c. 1906 to c. 1959, having been across the road for a few years before that. (See also page 32.)

Construction of the enlarged Green, May 1932. Frank Wells loaned this and the next view, which come from the same photograph. Bus 353 was a 1929 AEC Regent, that was withdrawn from service in 1950.

Laying the tram tracks at the new terminus, May 1932.

Alder's Garage, Warwick Road, c. 1929. Around 1933 Alder's let out the showrooms on both sides to four other businesses and built a row of shops to the right as well. Miss Elizabeth Pare's confectionery business at 1194 was hugely popular with schoolchildren! She ran it until 1963. W.N. Dixon moved into 1200. The butcher Leonard Wilkes at 1206 kept livestock behind his shop until the early 1960s. Alder's still own the whole row.

Dixon's, 1200-2 Warwick Road, c. 1933. The late Wilfred Norman Dixon described this as his mini department store. The display took two hours to put out, and was four yards deep. He became an extraordinarily successful businessman, opening ten units in Acocks Green alone and stores in other towns, all high class establishments which he ran himself. Apparently, Acocks Green was called 'Dixons Green' by some! The bonnet of his American car can just be seen on the left.

Dennetts Drapers, corner of Oxford Road, c. 1940. H. Westwood, farmer, lived here at the turn of the century, and from the 1901 directory John Bishop, draper, was in business. From c. 1910 to 1937 John Dennett ran the business. It was bought by Mr Benjamin Coulles in 1937, who continued to trade under the Dennetts name, adding his own name to it. They later bought the hairdresser's premises next door and began to sell ironmongery and hardware as well as drapery. Lino and carpets were added in 1949 and furniture in 1959. In 1965 they extended into their garden on Oxford Road. Eric Coulles took over in 1956 and Andrew Coulles in 1985. Dennetts is a rare survival: a family businesses of long standing.

Mr Benjamin Coulles demonstrating a vacuum cleaner to housewives in the Dolphin pub, c. 1953.

New shops at Shirley Road, February 1932. The signs say: This shop will shortly be opened for grocery and provisions, also boiled ham, al-a-mode beef [sic], sausage and brawn, milk, bread and confectionery and This shop will open Tuesday next, by C. Dexter, with fruit, vegetables, fish, rabbits etc., fresh daily.

Alfred Compton, stationmaster of Acocks Green and Olton, at Acocks Green, early 1950s.

The Birmingham Co-operative Society was expanding rapidly at the end of the 1920s. They opened their 100th store at Fox Hollies Road on 16 November 1929. Les and Mary Smith recall the manager, Mr Bradshaw and the cashier, Miss Hartill. Grocery and provisions, confectionery and butchery were at 295-9, and fish, fruit and greengrocery were at 285.

A Saltley Sanitary Steam Laundry van at Douglas Road, c. 1913. The house next to number 58 is being built.

Ethel Hone and Rosalind Williams at the Acocks Green and Olton Laundry, Warwick Road, c. 1942. The laundry began trading here c. 1902. Both ladies were clerks in the office, and Ethel Hone worked here from 1937-44. They are seated on a horse-drawn delivery van. Despite all the special presses, Ethel remembers a lot of hand finishing being done, for example the goffering of maids' caps. She also told me she took home a worn sheet of felt from a calender press used for sheets: this became a floorcovering in the front room of her house, and a Morrison indoor air-raid shelter was erected on top of it: this was a kind of reinforced large metal table with wire mesh sides to protect against flying debris.

The interior of the Co-op Laundry at the Vineries, reopening day, 13 July 1946. The laundry had first opened in February 1939. Even after losing part of the premises to the war effort, it still retained two hundred and fifty employees until April 1942, when the entire site was requisitioned for use by the Rover Aircraft Company, whose factory was nearby. The machines were removed to the bakery at Stechford. The new laundry was opened by the MP for Yardley, Mr Wesley Perrins. It contained a variety of presses apart from the ones seen here, specially shaped for collars, sleeves, and cuffs. Washing was separated on arrival, marked, washed, dried and ironed according to its needs and brought together again for packing in a highly organized operation. Extensive sports facilities were available in the grounds.

Electric laundry vans outside the Co-op Laundry, December 1948. The camouflage paint remained until the buildings were demolished. The laundry closed on 21 February 1975. A 1977 application for a superstore to be built here was turned down.

The Co-op's coal house at Yardley Road wharf, c. 1940.

Staffordshire coal being delivered at Yardley wharf on the canal at Acocks Green. The narrowboat is called *Here She Comes*. The BCS had acquired the wharf as early as 1912. Its coal department closed on 30 June 1979.

Kelsall's confectioners, 298 Fox Hollies Road, Silver Jubilee 1935 or Coronation 1937.

The smithy, Warwick Road on a card posted on 4 November 1908. This was opposite Stockfield Road (see page 44). It was built in the 1780s and was in business until c. 1949. Mary Smith recalls seeing horses shod when she went to her father's allotment behind here as a child. It was common for bakery vans, laundry vans, milk floats and coal waggons to be horse-drawn until well into the motor vehicle era. In fact the Co-op dairy did not finish with horses until c. 1960.

Road-making at Shaftmoor Lane, 8 July 1920. Lt.-Col. Walker's 1912 land purchase is on the right.

The Auxiliary Fire Service at Station Road, c. 1940. At the front on the left as we look is Jack Pitt and third from the right at the front is Brooke Oliver, local coal merchant. The AFS, which began in late 1937, was absorbed into the National Fire Service in 1941.

The National Fire Service at Acocks Green Fire Station, c. 1941. This station was open by the beginning of 1923, with a motor turbine pump and ladders. To make the station, various police officers had to lose the gardens outside their quarters at the back of the 1909 police station. Acocks Green fire station closed on 22 February 1993 and moved to Speedwell Road, very close to where the first local fire brigade came from. That was created in 1895 by Muscotts following a fire at their tannery. (Thanks to David Cross for help with this information.)

John Gilbert's prizewinning horse Christie on their Co-op milk round off Stockfield Road, 1953.

Christie at Kilmorie Road, 1953. This was the year he won 'best in his class' at the Birmingham Horse Show.

Five

Portraits

A wedding portrait at Spring Road, which is now part of Olton Boulevard East, c. 1920. The house was occupied by Joseph Smith, kennelmaster to Lt.-Col. Walker. This photograph was lent by Mrs Marjorie Davies, here the bridesmaid. She was five or six years old at the time: the wedding was of her aunt, Joseph Smith's daughter. Marjorie used to walk with Mary Walker carrying flowers to St Mary's church. This is where the Fox Hollies pub used to be.

Joseph Smith, kennelmaster to Lt.-Col. Walker. He worked for him for fifty years, dying early in 1930 at the age of 68. In 1909, when he was in charge of the mastiff dog kennels at Fox Hollies Hall, twenty-seven first prizes, six seconds, nine thirds, and many other awards were won. Eight championship wins in a row were achieved.

Mary Walker, c. 1920. She was Zaccheus Walker's sister, and lived with him at Fox Hollies Hall. She was a notable figure in the Guides, and was a familiar sight in Acocks Green in her open carriage with her parasol up. After her brother's death she moved to Sussex, where she died at the age of 92 in 1938. The story of the Walker family is fascinating. Revd Robert Walker of Seathwaite in the Lake District was described as 'the wonderful', and was mentioned in a poem by Wordsworth. His son Zaccheus I, a merchant, married a sister of Matthew Boulton. In the next generation Zaccheus II nearly lost his life in the French Revolution, but was saved by his friendship with Robespierre, whom he had met in the United States. His son Zaccheus III, Mary's and Zaccheus IV's father, was a successful merchant and it was he who bought the Fox Hollies estate.

The Westwood family, c. 1903. Joseph Westwood, on the right at the back, was the entrepreneur behind a chain of fruit and vegetable businesses in Springfield, Sparkhill, Sparkbrook and Bournbrook. He was a powerful figure in the retail fruit trade. In the back row on the left are Kate, then Gertrude, Margaret, Jessy and Joseph. In front are Phoebe, Josephine, Fred, Garnet, Ida, and Lincoln, with Molly in front of Phoebe. Kate married Thomas Coldrick, who helped Joseph to run the shops during World War I. They moved to the Vineries when it was bought by the Westwoods, by which time Thomas was a partner in the business. Later Tom Coldrick became an important figure in the Retail Fruiterers' Association in his own right, becoming President in 1937. (Thanks to Charles Coldrick for this information.)

Joseph Wheildon Izod and Fanny Sophia Izod, nee King, at Broomhall Farm, c. 1935. J.W. Izod sold seventeen acres adjoining the Walker estate for £3,290 on 28 August 1929: part of Broomhall Crescent and Gospel Farm Road cover the area. On 9 December 1931 he sold a further thirteen acres to the city for £2,500, much of which was used for the playing field behind Lakey Lane school, where anti-aircraft guns and a barrage balloon were stationed during the War. J.W. Izod died on 31 January 1942. His widow stayed on at Broomhall until after the War. Nearly twelve acres including the farmhouse were sold to the city on 21 February 1947 for £7,000, and the house was demolished. Prefabs were built at Lakefield Close: the name refers both to the moat and the Gaskell and Chambers sports field formerly rented from the Izods. The prefabs were later replaced. Edenbridge Road was extended over the rest of the area, c. 1951. The footpath from Lakey Lane through to Edenbridge Road is more or less on the line of the former drive to Broomhall. Fanny Izod and her brother Walter King had moved to their last piece of land nearby at Shirley Road at the time of the sale: the one acre field next to the cottage was sold on 25 June 1948 for £1,500. She lived on at Moorland Cottage until she died at the age of 99 in January 1973.

Fred Cowan Senior and his wife Evelyn, c. 1910. They got married on 11 June of that year.

Fred Cowan Junior as a little boy with his mother, c. 1917. Irene, his sister, who was born in 1911, married Edward Pitt.

Fred Cowan Senior in World War One (he is the man standing).

Fred Cowan Junior as a boy, c. 1925.

Fred Cowan Junior in World War II, 1940. He died in 1995, aged 81.

Bert Standley, c. 1910. He spent all his working life at Pitt's.

Bert's sister Edith Standley. As nurse Maund after marriage, she delivered over one thousand babies in Acocks Green. At first, she was able to bring mothers to her house, Ivycots on Hazelwood Road, for delivery and aftercare, but when the city required registration and inspection, she changed to staying in people's homes, usually for a month at a time.

Frank Wells as a young man, c. 1932. He is on the roof of the Warwick cinema, where he was rewind boy for three years from the age of sixteen.

Mary Tregenza at the age of eleven at Dryden Grove, Silver Jubilee of King George V, 1935.

The fun-loving girl has blossomed into a young woman, seen here in 1942 at her engagement to Les Smith, again at Dryden Grove. I have been fortunate to have had their kind and generous help during my researches for this book.

The Gloster family at the Croft, Yardley Road, 1906. Left to right they are Oscar, Martha, Joseph, Ernest, Frances, Joseph Junior, Martha Ann, Leonard, Sadie and Archibald. The Croft stood at the corner of Elmdon Road, next to Cottesbrook House. At the age of nine Joseph became an errand boy to Mr Oliver of Warstone Lane, engraver, and four years later he was apprenticed. Later he had his own silversmith's factory in Hockley. He became a JP for Worcestershire in 1909 and served on Yardley Rural District Council as Councillor and Chairman. After Birmingham absorbed Yardley, he was made an Alderman. He retired from politics in 1930 and died on 17 August 1944. His son Oscar, a solicitor, became a councillor in 1930, representing Acocks Green, and became an Alderman in 1949. He was President of the Acocks Green British Legion, and unveiled the Cenotaph at the library in August 1965.

Revd Frederick Thomas Swinburn, c. 1880. He was the first vicar of St Mary's, serving from 1867-90. In 1889 he was presented with a beautiful illuminated address expressing the gratitude of his parishioners, from which this portrait is taken (see also page 114 for another page from this address).

Revd Philip James Kelly. Ordained in 1905, he came to St Mary's on 20 June 1931. It was said that he ruined his health with overwork. He was unable to continue with his duties after December 1952. He left in 1953 and died in 1956. Interestingly, he was a controversial figure in the debates on temperance, challenging a teetotaller to a public debate in the Church Hall on 11 December 1946, where he argued that teetotalism and fanaticism fettered the gift of free will, which was strengthened by moderation and temperance. On 7 December 1943 he had held what seemed at the time an extraordinary service in the Dolphin, to honour the war dead relatives of customers, which he repeated annually and later conducted in the Great Western too (see page 116). He stated that he wanted to see the Word of God introduced into every public house in England. The Great Organ and a window in the north aisle of St Mary's are dedicated to his memory.

Dr Cordley Bradford, 1907. He was a major figure in Acocks Green and lived from c. 1880 in a large house called Merstowe, which stood on the Warwick Road near Broad Road. He was churchwarden for a quarter of a century at St Mary's from 1907, and a JP from 1909. He was a doctor for fifty-two years, making his rounds in a gig: he kept his horses in a field nearby. His family gave an organ screen in his memory in December 1933 and the congregation gave a baptistery screen and marble flooring in November 1936.

Very Revd Canon John Aloysius Gibbons, c. 1945. He was born on 26 June 1869 and came to Acocks Green from St Chad's on 10 August 1905, arriving at the same time as the nuns, and set about developing the Parish for the Roman Catholic community. He was made an Honorary Canon in 1941 and received the gift of a Monstrance in 1942. For his seventieth birthday he was presented with an illuminated address in the Public Hall, which was at the time his Parish Hall. He died on 18 November 1954 at the age of eighty-five.

Leonard Skan, milkman, with his horse, Peter, in the field at the corner of Flint Green Road in the 1930s.

Six

Schooldays

Boys at Acocks Green Convent School, 1914/15. The school was started in 1905 by nuns from the Order of Our Lady of Compassion, who came from Olton. They began in Wilton House, and moved in 1919 to the Hollies next door. The Wilton House site was used for the church. The convent school was sold to the church authorities in 1948 and it subsequently became a private school for boys from six to fourteen years called Crosby Hall.

Acocks Green Convent School, 1925. This first part of a panoramic photograph was found at a car boot sale in Weston super Mare by Ava Westwood!

Acocks Green Convent School, 1925, the next part of the group. This was a day and boarding school.

Acocks Green Convent School, 1925, the final part. Nearby was Holy Souls school, built in 1907 and extended in 1931 with a square addition on the front. The two schools operated alongside each other. Holy Souls was a mixed school for eight to fourteen year olds: younger boys went to the convent school. In the early 1950s Holy Souls was using a few prefabs in grounds behind Crosby Hall school. In the mid-1950s public money finally became available to help with the building of a 'Special Agreement' secondary school and Archbishop Ilsley school and grounds were built over the next few years. The old school is now an annexe. Wellesbourne school was purchased in 1966 and further extensions to Archbishop Ilsley school followed that same year, in 1970, from 1972-5 and from 1987-9. As part of a set of land deals, some land and Crosby Hall was sold by the church authorities for the Safeway/Red Lion redevelopment c. 1981.

Acocks Green School, Infants, 1913 or 1914. Note where the children have, presumably, been told to put their hands! The school was built in 1908.

Acocks Green School, c. 1917.

Acocks Green School, Infants Class 4, 1921.

Teachers at Acocks Green School, 1923. Connie Maund recalls their names. Back row, left to right: Miss Wardley, Miss Thomson, Miss Hill (Head), Miss Wood, Miss Driscoll (a pupil); front row: Miss Weeds, Miss Copeland, Miss Mills, Miss Edwards.

Acocks Green School, 1928.

Acocks Green School, 1929. Estella McAllister is at the left end of the third row from the back, and her twin brother John is at the left end of the row in front of her, as we view.

Acocks Green School, 1931. Mary Tregenza, later Smith, is third from the right in the front row as we look.

Acocks Green School, five year olds, 1931. Mary Millington, now Seaton, is second from the left on the back row. Other names she and Betty Harrison recall are: John Wright, Laurence Rushton, Gwyneth Creasey, Pauline Bolton, Mary Barnacle, and June Rainbow.

Acocks Green School, 1931.

Acocks Green Infants, 1933. This is Empire Day. John Wright, Betty Harrison (Seal then) and Mary Seaton (Millington then) recall: back row, left to right: John Wright, Kenneth Enstone, Betty Seal (playing Britannia), Joy Secret, Laurence Rushton. Second row: -?-, Jacqueline Bagshaw, Vera Brown, Mavis Cornelius, Winifred Terence, Barbara ?, -?-. Third row: -?- , Patricia Woodward, Donald Beddows, Mary Millington, Donald Ward, Harold Evans, John Rhodes.

Acocks Green Infants, 1933. Brothers and sisters were allowed to accompany their younger siblings here.

Acocks Green Junior, 1934. Some of the names are remembered by Betty Harrison and Mary Seaton. In the rows from back to front, left to right, they are: Laurence Rushton, Miss Neal, Donald Beddows; Kenneth Enstone, Patricia Woodward, Mary Millington, Joy Secret, Winifred Terence, Eileen Davis, Betty Seal; Gina Cadman, Mavis Cornelius, Jacqueline Bagshaw, June Davis, Hazel Nicholls; George Craig, Jean Bailey, Patricia Kedwards.

Acocks Green Junior, 1934. Mary Tregenza is fifth from the left in the second row from the back as we view.

Acocks Green Infants Parents' Day, 1935.

Reception class children dancing round the Maypole, Mrs Rabouhans' class, Acocks Green Infants, 1958.

Teachers at Acocks Green Infants School, 1961. Back row, left to right: Miss Maul, Mrs M. Newman, Mrs Joyce Beckett, Mrs D. Davies, Mrs D.M. Rabouhans. Front row: Miss Husband, Miss Leonard (Head), Miss Holder (Deputy Head).

Severne Road Council School, 1931.

The football team, Oaklands School, Dolphin Lane, 1957-8. The male teacher seated is Edward Palser (see page 126). The teacher on the left on the back row is Mr Lloyd.

Wellesbourne School football team, c. 1897. Mary Smith's father, Harry Tregenza, has the ball. The school operated from 1885 to 1966 as a private day school for boys from eight years old. The buildings still stand behind the 1907 Catholic school building on the Warwick Road, but are now offices. The grounds were sold off to the church authorities.

A concert party at St Mary's School, 1932. St Mary's church school opened at Broad Road on 23 February 1874, with a formal opening taking place on 10 March. It survived as a school until 1979 and is now a church. Ron Powell, who lent this photograph, is one of the group. He recalls being sent with a friend one day to Fox Hollies Hall to ask for a donation for the school.

Eastbourne House, Warwick Road. This was listed as a doctor's house until 1909. It stood not far beyond Station Road (see page 31). The Misses Marshall then took it over as a private school for girls, with preparatory age boys as well. It had a high reputation, and was fondly remembered. They left c. 1934, and the school moved to Dudley Park Road, where it remained until 1948. Eastbourne House was replaced by shops (see page 37).

Fernbank, Yardley Road, 1946. This classy house was finished on 25 March 1858 and was one of five mansions on the west side of Yardley Road. Alterations to the house were made c. 1880. It had tiles in two colours, green and dark blue, until a few years ago, when these and the decorative barge boards had to be replaced. At the time of the photograph the house was occupied by the Beckett family, who had a dry cleaning business. Fernbank was bought by Mr Frank Moynihan on 28 June 1948 for £4,250 as a new home for Eastbourne House School, which opened there in September. The school had become run down during the war and Mr Moynihan had taken it over two years earlier at Dudley Park Road. He revived its fortunes. There are large grounds behind, where Mr Moynihan took over facilities for animals and birds. He kept four to five hundred hens, three pigs and over one hundred pheasants there. His son Patrick, who succeeded him as owner, told me that his father came home a little the worse for wear one evening around 1960 and went to look at the pens. They received a call from the police next morning, asking if they had lost some pheasants. After checking the pens, which were open, they and George Perkins the chemist, their partner in breeding game, ran to the Green to find the traffic island heaving with the birds. Needless to say, they did not recover many! The school used to take one hundred and thirty pupils from three to eleven years. Private schools were very numerous locally at one time, and were an important part of the community. Indeed one former pupil said that Acocks Green would not be Acocks Green without Eastbourne House school. I would like to thank Patrick Moynihan for this information. Sadly, the school has now closed down.

Seven

Social Life

The Old Dolphin, publican Walter Pagett, c. 1905. This was the furthest point in Acocks Green until suburban developments late last century and the tollhouse and tollgate were between here and Woodcock Lane (Woodberry Walk). There was also a weighbridge here. The shops at Oxford Road can be seen on the right.

The Old Dolphin on a card posted on 16 January 1907. The hens and vehicles add considerable charm to the scene. This inn closed on 15 May 1930 and the licence was transferred the next day to the new Dolphin, which was built behind this one. This attractive inn had to go because the road was due to be widened, a process still not completed right through the village even now.

The new Dolphin, 1930. Even this new building was not secure for long. Brewers were under Government pressure to reduce the number of public houses around 1990, and this pub was replaced by an Aldi supermarket in 1991. Freda Cocks, later Lord Mayor, was licensee for some years until 1973.

The Spread Eagle, c. 1905. Matthew Bissell was the licensee. He liked to call the inn 'Ye Old Manor House'. It closed on 20 September 1928, and Mr Bissell and the licence went to the new Fox Hollies. Within a year or so the Spread Eagle was demolished for road widening. The site is in the carriageway at the pedestrian lights near Victoria Road.

The Red Lion, 14 July 1959. It was bought leasehold by M & B from John Rabone for £1,250 on 21 January 1891, then £13,750 was paid to W.T. Rabone for the freehold on 27 July 1931. This attractive pub was demolished in September 1982. The wood, rotten and infested, was put on a huge bonfire at Eastbourne House school. The new Red Lion was half built behind the old pub at this time, and was at first called the Trader.

The Fox Hollies, c. 1928. This was architecturally an extremely fine pub. It opened on 21 September 1928. It was designed for M & B in 1927 by Edwin F. Reynolds of Wood, Kendrick and Reynolds. If it appears that the building has the look of a country house, this is in fact true. Andy Foster, a noted conservationist, has seen a sketchbook belonging to the Reynolds family which shows a country house design of 1914 which is obviously the inspiration for the Fox Hollies. The bas-relief of fox and holly leaves was designed by William Bloye. Reynolds himself was a lecturer in architecture at the School of Art. Birmingham is important nationally in the history of pub architecture, developing a new style of 'reformed' inn, bright, airy and lofty, indeed a coaching inn for the road transport era, which would be usable by the whole family, with ample parking and gardens. The large and spacious interiors have also meant that these pubs could be remodelled internally to accommodate new trends in brewery marketing without the need for demolition. This led to some bizarre 'fun pubs' during the 1980s, with plastic and neon themed rooms inside a building which looks balanced and in good taste from the outside. Thankfully, that phase seems to have ended! Interestingly, the first plans for the Fox Hollies show the entrance facing the corner at Summer Road and the last stretch of Spring Road as it was then. The Fox Hollies has been replaced by a supermarket.

The Great Western, c. 1905. Situated right next to the station, and built very soon after it opened, this was the ideal place to wait for one's rail or carriage transport. It was sold to William Butler in 1895 by Mann, Crossman and Paulin, now part of Courage. (Eric Williamson informed me that the Great Western was rebuilt in 1956-1957 - he preferred the old one!)

The Britannia Inn, 1 November 1938. This turn of the century pub replaced an earlier small inn in the cottage row, listed in a directory of 1864. It was replaced in 1973. George Slack of Colliers told me that it was demolished and all the rubble was cleared away in just one day. He said it was as if the old Britannia had never existed, the work was so quick and complete.

The Picture Playhouse, corner of Station and Warwick Roads, c. 1914. The opening of this was reported in December 1913. It had 520 seats and only showed silent films. The management served tea to early arrivals! It closed in 1929 when the Warwick cinema opened on Westley Road, and was demolished by early 1935.

The Warwick Cinema, c. 1929. The interior was designed to look like the grounds of a medieval castle, hence the name. It opened on 16 September 1929, with 1,300 seats. It closed in 1962 for refurbishment as a bowling arcade and smaller cinema. The cinema did not reopen until 29 March 1964 and has been replaced by a laser combat business.

St Mary's church, c. 1900. The church was the outcome of meetings of local people in 1864. The site was given by Yardley Charity Trustees and John Field Swinburn gave an endowment of £1,000. The foundation stone was laid on 13 October 1864, and on 17 October 1866 a portion of the nave and two aisles were consecrated. A parish was created in 1867. Despite further periods of construction, by 1898 there were still no north and south transepts, Lady Chapel, choir vestry or tower.

St Mary's church and the churchyard, c. 1925. Note the roundel windows and the very steep pitch of the roof (see page 115). In 1928/9 a Memorial Hall was built on Summer Road near the bus garage, to be used for meetings, and in 1936 Bishop Westcott Hall was opened at the end of Greenwood Avenue.

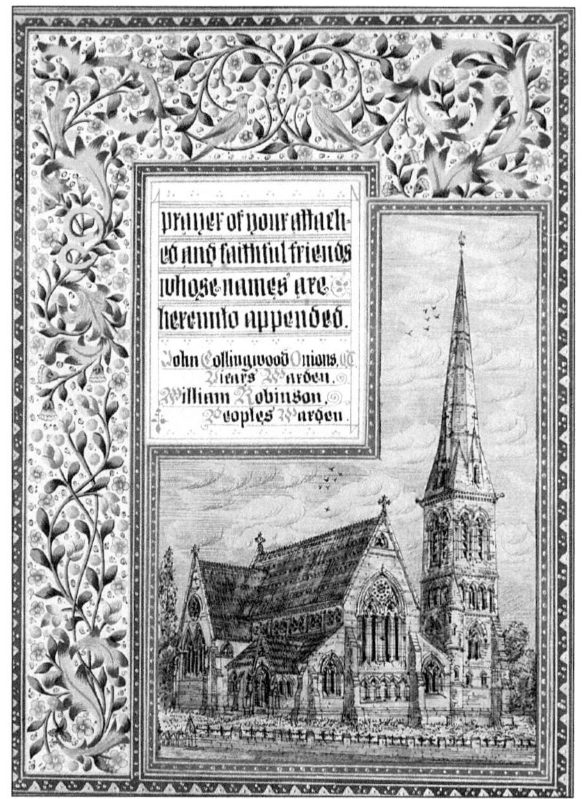

The tower and spire as originally planned. They were to be one hundred and sixty seven feet high. This page from an illuminated address (mentioned on page 90) shows what a dominant feature the church was originally intended to be.

The reredos and altar, St Mary's church, c. 1905. The 1898 altar is on steps of Devonshire marble. The reredos is of alabaster and was installed in 1903. The north wing was given by Revd James Balleine and the south wing by Dr and Mrs Cordley Bradford. The stained glass in the east window is from designs by Burne-Jones. It was erected in memory of Revd Frederick Swinburn in 1895 by his wife and son. At 8.20 p.m. on 10 December 1940 a bomb landed in the nave just in front of the lectern, blew this window out, and destroyed all the other stained glass in the church. Cyril Faulks, who helped me with this information, told me his confirmation class had just gone to the cellar of the vicarage. Revd Philip Kelly picked up the pieces of the east window and gave them to the Art Gallery for safe keeping.

Bomb damage, St Mary's, December 1940. Although the roof was blown off, and many internal features were destroyed, the structure was unaffected. Services were held elsewhere, including at the Warwick cinema, until Easter 1941, by which time the north aisle of the church had been roofed over, the space between the pillars had been boarded up, and a coke boiler put in at the back. Another service held at the Warwick cinema on 26 April 1942 attracted over 1,400 young people. After the war, the walls of the nave were raised to reduce the pitch of the roof, which had made repairs difficult and expensive, and larger clerestory windows replaced the original roundels. The new glass was not stained but clear, so the church became lighter. It was reconsecrated on 8 October 1949.

The vicarage gardens, c. 1930. The vicarage was built by February 1871. It was sold in 1974, together with its land, to the council for building purposes. The vicarage moved to Dudley Park Road. Unfortunately, St Mary's was thereby deprived of a site for car parking and meeting rooms.

The Church House, on the corner of Arden Road and Rockwood Road, c. 1908. This was one of several buildings owned by St Mary's in the past. A mission room had opened at Spring Road in 1881, which moved to Summer Road in 1905, as it was in the way of the coming North Warwickshire railway line. The mission room was replaced by a Memorial Hall in 1928/9, but that was later sold to ROSPA. Bishop Westcott Hall was opened in 1936 at the end of Greenwood Avenue: it is now used by the city council for Fox Hollies Forum. The Church House was occupied by the Birmingham City Mission by 1983, for use as a training and voluntary work centre for the unemployed.

Revd Philip Kelly conducting one of the annual Remembrance Services, here at the Great Western Hotel, c. 1950 (see page 91).

A sale of work at St Mary's, July 1938. Back row, left to right: Revd F.E. Compton, Mrs Wood, Revd P.J. Kelly, Mrs Tardan, Mr Nicols and Revd B.P. Evans. Front row: Mrs P.J. Kelly, Mrs A.W. Adams, Miss Burrows, Mrs Nicols, with Miss Brown in front. On 22 September 1939 just seven and a half hours elapsed between proposal and solemnization of marriage for Mr and Mrs T.G. Franklin at St Mary's. This used to be in the Guinness Book of Records as the fastest white wedding of all time.

The Methodist church, Shirley Road and the original manse, seen from Botteville Road, 1912.

The Methodist church, c. 1905. Worship has been traced locally to the 1850s. The first chapel dates from 1863 and is the section visible here with a cross in the gable. A schoolroom and other rooms were built on in 1872, and the left-hand section is the new Gothic-style church, which was built alongside in 1882, with the old chapel becoming a schoolroom. In 1895 the house next to the church on Botteville Road was bought as a manse. In 1927 the church was enlarged to incorporate the school as a transept and side-aisle. Revd G.B. Robson felt so glad to be getting rid of the 'over-fussy' original features at this time that he heaved a half-brick through the 'preposterous fancy window' facing Shirley Road! A school and Institute were added at the back in place of the manse and another house, opening on 9 December 1933. In the meantime the Sunday School had had to go to the council schools at Westley/Warwick Roads. Social life at the church was extraordinarily successful: for example, the Guild had literary, arts, crafts, musical, photographic and other similar activities. Special mention must be made of the initiative which began at the same time as the 1927 extension, and was prompted by the same thing: the building of the council estates. In 1927 the 'ladies' visited one thousand new houses in order to recruit members for a 'Women's Cheerful Hour'. This lasted for no less than fifty years from 1928, and one element of the work was the provision of a Maternity Bag to mothers, which had to be returned after one month. The church had taken over the former Temperance Institute in Westley Road near the school in August 1918 and used it as a social club until November 1933: it was known as the 'Tin Tab' and Sunday services were held there during the 1927 extensions. In 1971 a financial crisis prompted by reduced income from investments forced the church to let the buildings behind the church out on a long lease. The Sunday school and other activities had to go back into the church, so the nave was divided, with the church reopening on 9 June 1973.

The R.C. chapel in the extended greenhouse at Wilton House, Warwick Road, c. 1905. Nuns from the Order of Our Lady of Compassion arrived from Olton in 1905 at Wilton House and Father John Gibbons came very shortly afterwards. Two years later a building with a chapel upstairs and a school downstairs was opened nearby on the Warwick Road. In 1919 the nuns moved to the Hollies next door, and a church dedicated to the Sacred Heart of Jesus for the Deliverance of the Holy Souls in Purgatory was erected on the site of Wilton House. Half of the planned church was built and opened in 1925. It was completed in 1940 and consecrated on 24 October 1945.

Laying the foundation stone of the church, 18 April 1923. The church was also intended to be a memorial to and a shrine of prayer for the victims of war and the Army were represented here and in 1925.

The Archbishop of Birmingham, the Most Revd John McIntyre, DD, at the opening of the 'Eastern Market' at Acocks Green, 12 October 1927. This probably took place at the Public Hall and may well have been a fund-raising venture.

The Baptist church hall, Alexander Road, c. 1903. This first building of September 1903 was augmented by a new church in February 1914 and a new hall for the Sunday school in February 1925, which was used as a council school from 1930-3, until Yardley Road council school opened in huts across the road that were only recently replaced. In 1949 the school began to use the hall again.

The Congregational church, corner of Warwick and Stockfield Roads, c. 1905. Congregationalists were in the area by 1808 and opened a chapel on Rushall Lane (Stockfield Road) in 1827. This still stands, occupied by a business. The church itself opened on 20 June 1860. It was extended in 1895 and new schoolrooms were built alongside. Meanwhile, the former chapel had been used as a nonconformist school until 1884 and again from 1891-2 as a Board school. Joseph Gloster was a deacon here for many years (see page 90). The church closed in 1956 and was sold to the Bible Pattern Church Fellowship, becoming known as Warwick Road City Temple. It was demolished c. 1970 and the site is now part of Colliers.

The interior of the Congregational church, c. 1905.

The Christadelphian meeting hall, Station Road, 1912. Before the hall was built, Christadelphians met at the Public Hall.

The opening of Acocks Green Library, 14 June 1932. At the time, it was the biggest branch library to be opened in the city. It issued over nine thousand books in the first week. The iron railings were removed in the war, but were never used for the war effort. A Cenotaph and a turved memorial garden were provided by the British Legion in 1965. The walls have been reduced further and the frontage landscaped since then and a ramp has been provided on the left-hand side. (Thanks to Eddie Greaves for help with this information.)

Acocks Green Library, 14 June 1932. The screen on the left was removed and this magazine room was incorporated into the lending department after only a handful of years, in order to house more shelving for a larger bookstock. This very early alteration in the original design was matched by later changes to accommodate new services. There was a reading room across the hall, which has been a community room for meetings since the late 1970s. In October 1978 a drop-in centre for elderly people began in there, which still attracts up to one hundred people twice a week. In June 1987 the CAB began a weekly session in the room, as it was accessible for people with disabilities. This service operated for nearly a decade until their own premises in Station Road were extended. A major refurbishment, long planned and hoped for, finally began at the end of 1994, thanks to the city council, who provided the necessary capital funds at a very difficult time. True to the traditions of public service, the library stayed open until almost the end of the building operations in conditions which were at times most unpleasant for staff and public alike. After three weeks closure to finish off, the library reopened on 9 May 1995. The best of the original oak shelving, screening, panelling, and furniture has been retained. Most importantly a bright and colourful children's library has been provided, which was lacking before. The community room has been given a new kitchen, storeroom, toilet and parent and baby facilities, with new oak doors, skirting and fascias included to match the original detailing. The grandeur of the interior of the library, which was obscured by the large quantity of high shelving, is now apparent. Meetings, lectures, events and concerts take place there: it is a major cultural and information centre for the people of Acocks Green and beyond.

Acocks Green Institute, c. 1905. It was built in 1879. The Deed of Trust for the Institute, dated 1 July 1881, stated that it existed 'for the promotion of science, literature, the fine arts, the extension of literary, artistic and scientific knowledge and improvements in public speaking and debating and the provision of wholesome recreation for the members by means of lectures, concerts, miscellaneous entertainments, classes in various branches of education, essays and debates and a library of reference and circulation'. It was also used for meetings of Yardley District Council and as a magistrates court. Famous speakers came, including Sir Benjamin Stone and Oscar Wilde. It was sold in 1962 and demolished a few years later.

St Mary's Sunday school outing to Coleshill Park, 1922.

An outing leaving from outside Fred's Cafe, 1920s.

Acocks Green Laundry's float at a carnival, 1930s.

Acocks Green Woodcraft Folk on an outing at Yarningale Common, 5 May 1946. This is a group allied to the Co-operative Movement and its principles are co-operation, equality, democracy and peace. The Acocks Green 'Leaping Flame' group was formed c. 1943. At the time it met at Dolphin Lane School (Oaklands). Edward Palser (see page 104) and his wife Olive were leaders for some years. Among the boys are Moose (Raymond Cope), who has a beret, and Arthur Kesterton, who is the left-hand one of the two kneeling boys as we look. (Thanks to Olive Palser for this information.)

King George V Silver Jubilee celebrations at Dryden Grove, 1935. Third from the left in the back row as we view is Harry Tregenza, fourth is Mrs Tregenza, fifth is Frank Tregenza, Mary's brother.

George VI Coronation celebrations, 1937. The Hollyhock Road parade is leaving Eastcote Road.

Avondale Football Club, 1920s. This club played on a field behind Shirley Road at the village, where two short shop rows in mock-Tudor style were built in the early 1930s. Fred Cowan Senior was manager, according to his grand-daughter Dianne Kenny. He is second from the left in the second row from the back. He also had a tea stall by the pitch (see pages 67 and 85-7).

A fancy dress dance to raise funds for Avondale Football Club at the Public Hall, 1920s. The organiser is Alfred Wells, the man in the centre at the front (see page 66).

Ladies from Jack and Joan Cooper's Academy, 60 Shirley Road, 1942. This was a school of theatrical training, which operated here until 1964. Their wartime show, the 'Kabaret Follies' was very popular. The Academy supplied troupes of young ladies for pantomimes all over the country, troupes for shows at resorts, and dancers for revues and circuses.